# The World's First
# WOMEN
# DOCTORS

ELIZABETH BLACKWELL AND
ELIZABETH GARRETT A

Written by Isabel T

D1612671

## Collins

# A WORLD WITHOUT WOMEN

Two hundred years ago, the world of
medicine was a very strange place:

- Doctors treated patients
  by letting **leeches** suck
  their blood!
- Few people
  believed that germs
  caused disease!
- Women were not
  allowed to
  be doctors!

If you visit a doctor today,
you're equally likely to be
seen by a man or a woman.

Just before Queen Victoria came to the throne, two girls were born who would change medicine forever. Elizabeth Blackwell and Elizabeth Garrett Anderson grew up 3,500 miles and 15 years apart. But they shared the same goal: to train as doctors.

Elizabeth Garrett Anderson (1836–1917) was Britain's first woman doctor.

Elizabeth Blackwell (1821–1910) was America's first woman doctor.

At the time, this seemed impossible. Most people believed that women's brains and bodies were too weak to learn about medicine. Blackwell and Garrett Anderson set out to prove the world wrong.

# NOT IN THE CLUB

Elizabeth Blackwell and Elizabeth Garrett Anderson grew up in the early 1800s, when the idea of training women to be doctors was unthinkable. There were no women engineers, lawyers or scientists. Women weren't even allowed to **vote**.

## 2700 BCE

Queen Merit-Amon (also known as Merit Ptah) is the earliest female doctor on record. Her tomb describes her as "Chief Physician".

## 300 BCE

Metrodora was a Greek doctor. She was very good at treating women's diseases, and wrote the earliest surviving book by a female doctor.

The world had not always been this way. **Archaeologists** have found paintings and inscriptions that show women worked as doctors in ancient Egypt, almost 5,000 years ago. Until the Middle Ages, there were women doctors in Europe, too.

## 300 CE

In ancient Greece, Agnodice disguised herself as a man so she could help women give birth. When she was found out, her patients supported her. The law was changed to let women doctors treat other women.

## 1050 CE

Many women studied and taught at Salerno medical school in Italy. One of the most famous was Trotula, who wrote books to share her knowledge. One of her books was used to train doctors for hundreds of years.

# Amazing Nurses and Midwives

During the 12th century, many new universities opened in Europe. From then on, only people who had studied medicine at university were allowed to call themselves doctors, and women were banned from universities.

Women had begun working as nurses in hospitals during the 11th century, but during the Middle Ages, conditions were terrible, and nursing became seen as a job for women who had no other choices. Things began to improve in the 1600s and 1700s, and some women used their roles as nurses or midwives to make important improvements in healthcare.

However, by the 1800s, **midwifery** and nursing were still seen as roles for poor women. The Industrial Revolution was making the middle classes richer, and values were changing too. Middle-class women were not supposed to work.

This was bad news for patients. There were no doctors like Trotula and Metrodora, collecting knowledge about women's illnesses. **Modesty** also meant that women were less likely to visit doctors when they fell ill – instead, they suffered in silence.

In the 1800s, women received very little education. This led to claims that their brains were too weak to understand subjects such as medicine.

# HOW TO BUILD A PIONEER

In the early 1800s, the "normal" path for middle-class girls was to get married and have children. Work was seen as unladylike. Luckily, Elizabeth Blackwell and Elizabeth Garrett Anderson were born into families that weren't afraid to do things differently.

## MEET THE BLACKWELLS

Elizabeth Blackwell was born in Bristol, England, in 1821. Her family moved to the USA when she was eleven. Samuel Blackwell, Elizabeth's father, always tried to do the right thing, even if it made him unpopular. He didn't allow his daughters to do **frivolous** things such as wear pretty clothes, or learn how to sew. Instead, they grew up meeting interesting people and **campaigning** against slavery.

# MEET THE GARRETTS

Elizabeth Garrett Anderson was born in 1836, and grew up near the seaside in Suffolk, England. Her father Newson Garrett wanted to give his sons *and* his daughters a good education. Garrett Anderson spent two years at boarding school, and kept studying after she left. By the time she was 16, Elizabeth knew that she wanted to work for a living.

Elizabeth Blackwell and Elizabeth Garrett Anderson both had lots of brothers and sisters. Many of their siblings also grew up to do amazing things. Emily Blackwell became a pioneering doctor. Millicent Garrett helped to win women the right to vote.

# Feeling trapped

As teenagers, both Elizabeth Blackwell and Elizabeth Garrett Anderson began to worry about the next stage of their lives. They didn't feel excited about the "normal" path ahead.

## The expected paths in the 1800s

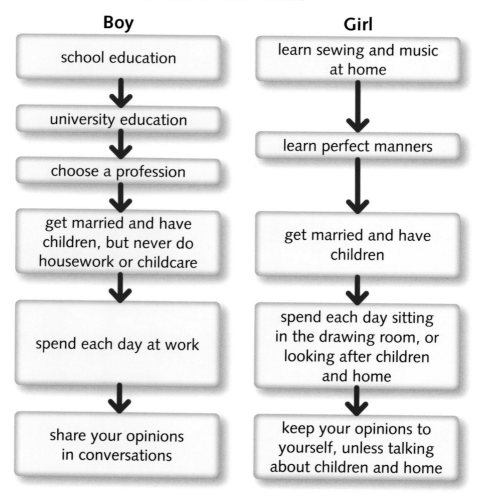

**Boy**
- school education
- university education
- choose a profession
- get married and have children, but never do housework or childcare
- spend each day at work
- share your opinions in conversations

**Girl**
- learn sewing and music at home
- learn perfect manners
- get married and have children
- spend each day sitting in the drawing room, or looking after children and home
- keep your opinions to yourself, unless talking about children and home

Many women, such as Florence Nightingale, felt the same as Blackwell and Garrett Anderson.

"What have I done this last fortnight? I have read to father ... learnt seven tunes by heart, written various letters. Ridden with Papa. Paid eight visits. Done company. And that is all ... And twenty or thirty years more to do thus!"

Florence Nightingale's diary, 1846

## DECIDING TO BECOME DOCTORS

Blackwell could not see how she would fit into the world in the way that women were supposed to. She hated housework and childcare. She hated the way people frowned on her for speaking her mind. Blackwell tried being a schoolteacher, but she hated that too.

"I really could not help crying upstairs when I thought of my situation. I know it is very wrong to be so ungrateful and I try very hard to be thankful but when I think of the long dreary years ahead I cannot always help it."

Elizabeth Blackwell's diary, aged 18

One day, a very ill friend told Elizabeth Blackwell that she had been too embarrassed to seek help from a male doctor. She suggested that Blackwell study medicine, so she could help other women.

> "If I could have been treated by a lady doctor, my worst sufferings would have been spared me."
>
> Elizabeth Blackwell's friend

At first Blackwell thought this was a horrible idea. She hated thinking about sickness and disease. But she was very taken with the idea that women should be able to visit female doctors if they wanted to. Blackwell decided this was the challenge she'd been looking for.

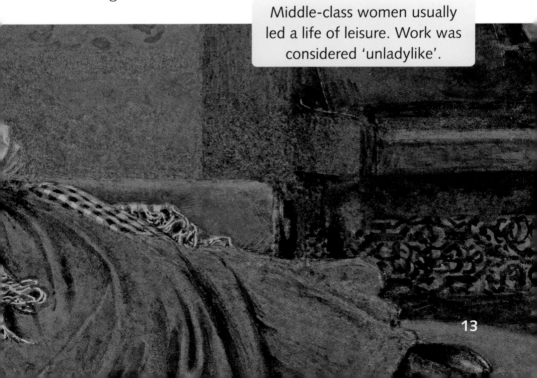

Middle-class women usually led a life of leisure. Work was considered 'unladylike'.

# FOLLOWING IN BLACKWELL'S FOOTSTEPS

As a teenager, Elizabeth Garrett Anderson and her friends thought it was unfair that men could work, rule and vote, but women were only allowed to be wives and mothers. But like Elizabeth Blackwell, Garrett Anderson did not think about becoming a doctor until someone else suggested it.

Elizabeth Blackwell was 15 years older than Garrett Anderson, and by 1859 she was already famous as America's first female doctor. Garrett Anderson was 23 when she heard that this amazing woman was visiting London. Her father arranged for the women to meet, and Blackwell encouraged Garrett Anderson to become a doctor too.

Elizabeth Garrett had to take a chaperone when she visited London, even though she was in her 20s.

At first Garrett Anderson panicked – she didn't think she was clever or special enough to be Britain's first female doctor. But she soon decided it would be an interesting and useful way to spend her life.

However, Elizabeth's parents were shocked and upset. She won her father over by explaining that she "could not live without some real work."

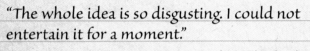

*"The whole idea is so disgusting. I could not entertain it for a moment."*

Newson Garrett, when Elizabeth told him she wanted to study medicine

# THE BATTLE BEGINS

Elizabeth Blackwell began her journey in America in 1844. She wrote to doctors and medical schools to ask how a woman could train as a doctor.

Each time she got the same reply: "It's impossible". One said that Blackwell would only be able to study medicine if she disguised herself as a man! Blackwell did not give up. She began working as a teacher to save money for her training. In her spare time, she read medical books and took private lessons.

Blackwell's lucky break came when she applied to Geneva College in New York. The head of the college felt bad about turning her down without a good reason, so he decided to let the students vote. The students thought it would be funny to say yes, and Blackwell got the acceptance letter she'd been waiting three years for.

In November 1847, Blackwell began life a student doctor.

Elizabeth Blackwell's acceptance letter to study medicine at Geneva College

# MINI-BIOGRAPHY:
# MARGARET BULKLEY (1795–1865)

Margaret Bulkley disguised herself as a man for 46 years, so she could train and work as a doctor in the early 1800s. "James Barry" had a reputation for being a fierce but very good doctor, and even became a hospital inspector. The truth was only discovered when "James" died.

Margaret Bulkley/James Barry is on the left.

## Breaking down barriers in Britain

Fast-forward to 1859, when Newson Garrett finally agreed to help his daughter meet doctors and apply to British medical schools.

Like Elizabeth Blackwell, Elizabeth Garrett Anderson faced rejection after rejection. Some doctors said, "Why not be a nurse?" "Because I prefer to earn a thousand, rather than twenty pounds a year," Garrett Anderson replied. The more rejections she got, the more determined she became.

Eventually, doctors at London's Middlesex Hospital agreed to let her work as a nurse, and study medicine in her spare time. Garrett Anderson soon won the respect of the doctors, and was allowed to attend classes with the male medical students.

Many people thought that a woman would faint or panic if she watched operations. In fact, Elizabeth enjoyed learning about the human body by **dissection**.

For a year everything seemed to go well. Then trouble began. Some of the other students were jealous of Garrett Anderson. One day she embarrassed them by answering a question none of them could get right. The angry students demanded that the hospital stop teaching her – and they won.

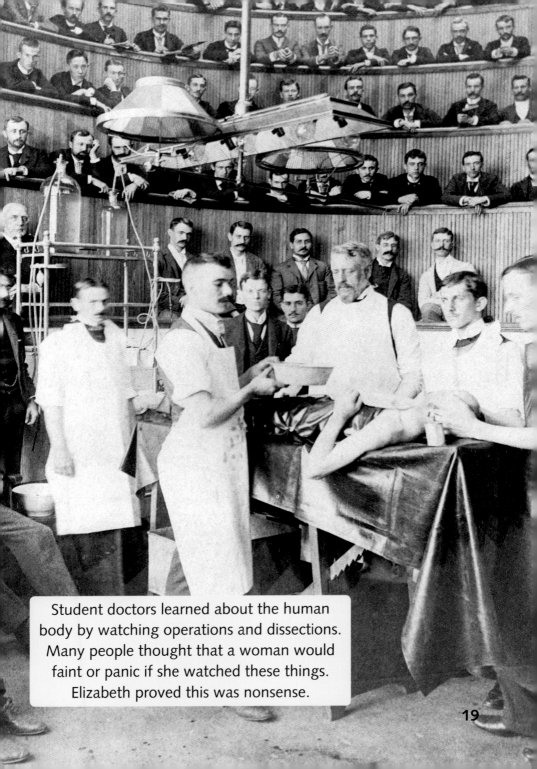

Student doctors learned about the human body by watching operations and dissections. Many people thought that a woman would faint or panic if she watched these things. Elizabeth proved this was nonsense.

**19**

Elizabeth Garrett Anderson had to leave Middlesex Hospital without a degree. She was heartbroken, but she vowed to keep going. She kept studying and applying to every medical school in the country. But it seemed hopeless – no British university would let her sit their exams.

Finally Garrett Anderson found a way in. The Society of Apothecaries had a rule that said they would give a **medical licence** to "all persons" who trained with a doctor for five years, and then passed its exams. Garrett Anderson argued that she was a "person", so by law, they had to let her sit the exams!

The Society agreed, hoping that she would go away and forget about it. Instead, Garrett worked hard to find doctors who would help her complete her training.

Apothecaries were a bit like today's GPs – patients came to them for medicines and general medical advice. Garrett Anderson actually wanted to be a hospital doctor, but this was a way to get the licence she needed to practise medicine.

In America, Elizabeth Blackwell's training had been much shorter, but just as tough. When she arrived in Geneva to start medical school, the town was shocked and suspicious – what kind of woman would dare to try and be a doctor?

At first the other students were just as rude, but Blackwell impressed them with her clever mind and calm nature. She soon proved that she was just a normal person who wanted to become a doctor.

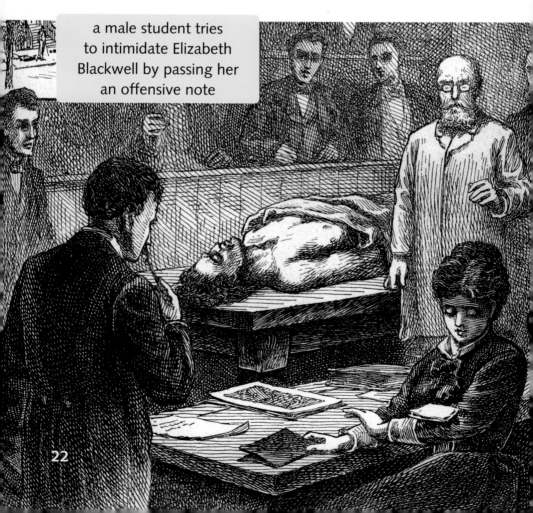

a male student tries to intimidate Elizabeth Blackwell by passing her an offensive note

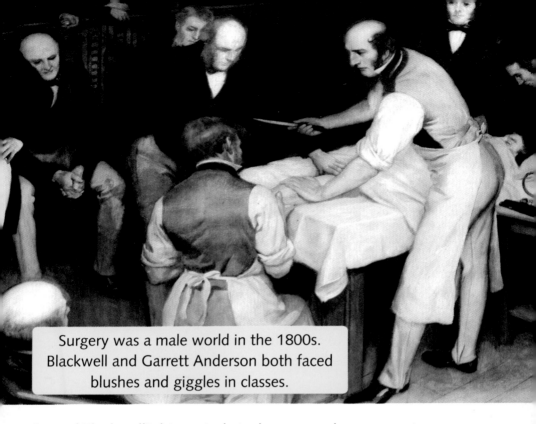

Surgery was a male world in the 1800s. Blackwell and Garrett Anderson both faced blushes and giggles in classes.

One of Blackwell's biggest obstacles was embarrassment. Learning about **anatomy** was an important part of becoming a doctor, but male teachers and students were embarrassed to talk about bodies in front of a woman.

Like Garrett Anderson, Blackwell was asked to stay away from dissection and anatomy lessons, but she talked her way back in. She didn't want to miss any of the training.

After two years, Blackwell had finished her course. It was time for the final exam.

# PRAISE ... AND PANIC!

In 1849, Elizabeth Blackwell passed her exams with the best marks in her class. She was the first woman in the world with a medical degree.

The news of Blackwell's success spread quickly. Many people were impressed, and excited about the future for women. Medical colleges received a wave of applications from women hoping to follow in Blackwell's footsteps, and during the 1850s ten more US medical colleges accepted their first female students. Several women-only medical schools also opened in America to meet the demand.

At her graduation ceremony, Blackwell told the college, "It shall be the effort of my life to shed honour upon your diploma."

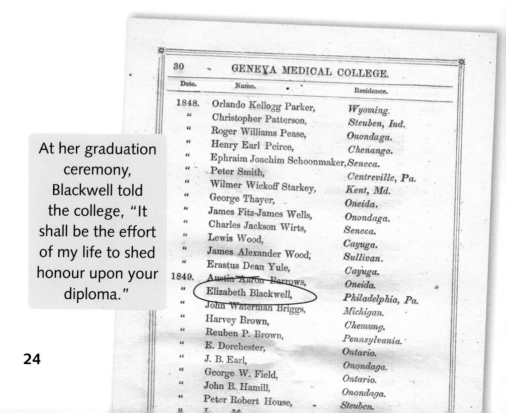

| 30 | GENEVA MEDICAL COLLEGE. | |
|---|---|---|
| Date. | Name. | Residence. |
| 1848. | Orlando Kellogg Parker, | Wyoming. |
| " | Christopher Patterson, | Steuben, Ind. |
| " | Roger Williams Pease, | Onondaga. |
| " | Henry Earl Peirce, | Chenango. |
| " | Ephraim Joachim Schoonmaker, | Seneca. |
| " | Peter Smith, | Centreville, Pa. |
| " | Wilmer Wickoff Starkey, | Kent, Md. |
| " | George Thayer, | Oneida. |
| " | James Fitz-James Wells, | Onondaga. |
| " | Charles Jackson Wirts, | Seneca. |
| " | Lewis Wood, | Cayuga. |
| " | James Alexander Wood; | Sullivan. |
| " | Erastus Dean Yule, | Cayuga. |
| 1849. | Austin Aaron Barrows, | Oneida. |
| " | Elizabeth Blackwell, | Philadelphia, Pa. |
| " | John Waterman Briggs, | Michigan. |
| " | Harvey Brown, | Chemung. |
| " | Reuben P. Brown, | Pennsylvania. |
| " | E. Dorchester, | Ontario. |
| " | J. B. Earl, | Onondaga. |
| " | George W. Field, | Ontario. |
| " | John B. Hamill, | Onondaga. |
| " | Peter Robert House, | Steuben. |

Young ladies all, of every clime,
Especially of Britain,
Who wholly occupy your time
In novels or in knitting
Whose highest skill is but to play,
Sing, dance, or French to clack well,
Reflect on the example, pray,
Of excellent Miss Blackwell!

This is part of a poem published in Punch magazine in 1865.

However, news of Blackwell's achievement did not please everyone. The Boston Medical and Surgical Journal called Blackwell's graduation a "farce", and asked doctors to make sure it didn't happen again. Geneva Medical School was embarrassed, and changed its rules to keep other women out.

## PLUCK AND PERSEVERANCE

Some people said that no other woman would be clever enough to follow in Elizabeth Blackwell's footsteps. They were wrong. In the USA, dozens of women began applying to medical school.

Sixteen years later in England, Elizabeth Garrett Anderson passed the Society of Apothecaries' exams, becoming the first women in Britain with a medical licence.

People were full of praise. The British Medical Journal said that "everyone must admire" Garrett Anderson's pluck and **perseverance**. But there was also criticism. And just like Geneva College, the Society of Apothecaries changed their rules to stop other women following Garrett Anderson's lead.

---

### Strange worries about female doctors
– Women weren't as clever as men.
– Women could not cope with stress.
– It would be improper for women to treat men.
– Men would stop respecting women.
– If women worked, there would be no one to raise
   children and create happy homes for their husbands.

Cruel cartoons made fun of a world where men and women swapped roles.

# HANDS-ON EXPERIENCE

As soon as they qualified, Elizabeth Blackwell and
Elizabeth Garrett Anderson faced a new battle.
They needed experience in treating patients, but no
hospital would employ a woman doctor.

## A DOCTOR IN PARIS

When Blackwell was rejected by American hospitals,
she decided to finish her training in Paris, France.
In the 1800s, it was the best place in the world to learn
about medicine. But in France, Blackwell was not famous.
No one seemed to care about her medical degree.
Once more, she was told to dress as a man!

Eventually, Blackwell found a way in. She joined
the trainee midwives at La Maternité – a huge hospital
where 3,000 babies were born each year. It was not
the role she had wanted, but it gave her a chance to work
alongside doctors and learn from them. Like all the other
trainees, she slept in a dormitory, shared a bath and
had no time to herself, but Blackwell enjoyed the work.
The doctors gave her more and more responsibility,
and she planned to become "the first lady surgeon in
the world".

Nineteenth-century Paris had the world's best hospitals.

## DISASTER STRIKES

One day, Blackwell caught a terrible eye infection as she was treating a baby. The doctors at La Maternité tried everything, but Blackwell was left blind in one eye. Her dream of becoming a surgeon was over.

In the 1800s, the medicines we use today had not yet been invented. The doctors tried these strange things to cure Blackwell's eye infection:

- eyelids burnt with a hot tool

- leeches stuck on her forehead

- poisonous plants smeared on her face

- footbaths

- mixture of clay and mustard spread on her face

- only allowed to eat broth.

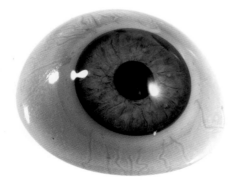

Elizabeth wore a fake eye for the rest of her life.

# MARY EDWARDS WALKER (1832–1919)

Mary Edwards Walker applied to medical schools as soon as she heard about Blackwell's graduation. She was eventually accepted at Syracuse Medical College, and graduated in 1855. She began working as a doctor, but patients stayed away. In 1861, Mary was refused a dangerous job as an army surgeon, so Mary volunteered as a nurse and began helping the male doctors. She was so good, that she was made assistant surgeon in 1862 – the first female surgeon in the USA.

Mary Walker, the only female assistant surgeon during the Civil War, was awarded the Medal of Honor in 1865. She broke away from traditional fashion and wore men's clothing.

Elizabeth Blackwell was heartbroken, but she decided to become a different kind of doctor. In 1851, she moved back to America and set up her own doctors' practice to give advice to patients. At first, it seemed that everyone was against her.

Although Blackwell had a degree and hospital experience, she was not allowed to put up a sign saying she was a doctor. In the first year, hardly any patients came to see her. Even women said the idea of a lady doctor was "horrid". Blackwell was poor, lonely, and unhappy. But she kept going, and things began to change.

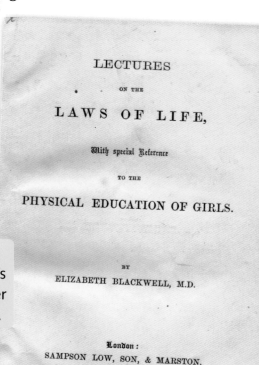

Blackwell began teaching about women's health, which helped her to attract new patients.

LECTURES

ON THE

LAWS OF LIFE,

With special Reference

TO THE

PHYSICAL EDUCATION OF GIRLS.

BY

ELIZABETH BLACKWELL, M.D.

London:
SAMPSON LOW, SON, & MARSTON,
CROWN BUILDINGS, 188, FLEET STREET.
1871.

In 1853, Elizabeth Blackwell managed to raise enough money to open a tiny clinic in New York City. She offered free medical advice to poor patients. In the first year, she saw more than 200 women.

This image of New York City from 1856 shows what the city would have looked like when Elizabeth Blackwell opened her clinic.

Running the clinic helped Blackwell to learn more about medicine and women's health. Her reputation grew and grew. In 1857, she opened the first hospital run for women, by women – the New York **Infirmary** for Women and Children. This was a big step. Although some women had been admitted to US medical schools by then, women had never before been allowed to practise medicine in any American hospital.

Many people said the hospital was doomed to fail. But Blackwell managed to win enough support and funding to prove them all wrong. The Infirmary treated thousands of patients in its first year.

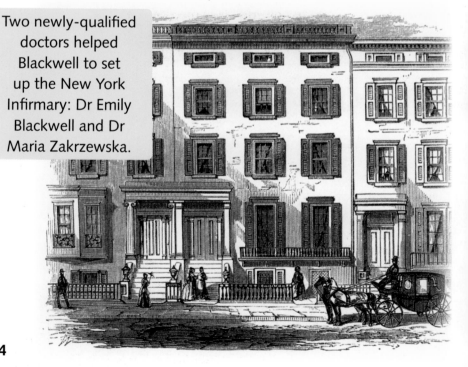

Two newly-qualified doctors helped Blackwell to set up the New York Infirmary: Dr Emily Blackwell and Dr Maria Zakrzewska.

# MINI-BIOGRAPHY:
# EMILY BLACKWELL (1826–1910)

Blackwell's sister Emily got a medical degree in 1854,
and spent two years working as a doctor in Europe.
When she came back to America,
Emily helped her sister open
the New York Infirmary.
Emily was the surgeon, and
later ran the hospital for
40 years.

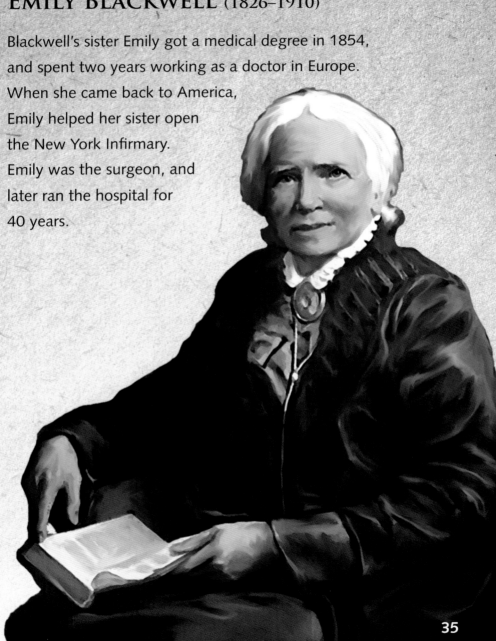

Elizabeth Garrett Anderson set up her first private practice in 1865, as soon as she gained her Society of Apothecaries' licence. Unlike Blackwell, she had plenty of money from her rich family, and a wide circle of female friends who believed in equal rights for women, and became her patients straight away.

But Garrett Anderson shared Blackwell's dream of working in a hospital, where she could treat all kinds of diseases and learn as much as possible. No hospital would give her a job, so in 1866 she set up her own clinic.

St Mary's Dispensary was a big success. It grew into England's first hospital for women and children. In 1874, the hospital moved to new buildings designed by Garrett Anderson. She was the hospital's surgeon for 20 years.

Newson Garrett helped his daughter raise the money to open St Mary's Dispensary in London. It opened during a **cholera** outbreak. People were too busy trying to get treatment to object to a woman doctor.

# TRAINING OTHER WOMEN

By the late 1850s, several hundred American women had followed Elizabeth Blackwell's lead and studied for a medical degree.

However, women medical students were not getting the same standard of training as men – even if they studied at the same institutions. The very best medical colleges still wouldn't let women in. Blackwell was worried that poor training would give women doctors a bad name.

In 1868, Blackwell opened her own medical school, joined to her hospital. The Women's Medical College of the New York Infirmary was the first medical school to make students study for four years. It also taught **hygiene**, which many male doctors were still ignoring.

## WHY WAS A DEGREE SO IMPORTANT?

Blackwell and Garrett Anderson knew that women doctors would not be taken seriously unless they studied the same courses and sat the same exams as men doctors. Garrett Anderson took her exams at a French university and returned to England with a medical degree from one of the best medical schools in the world.

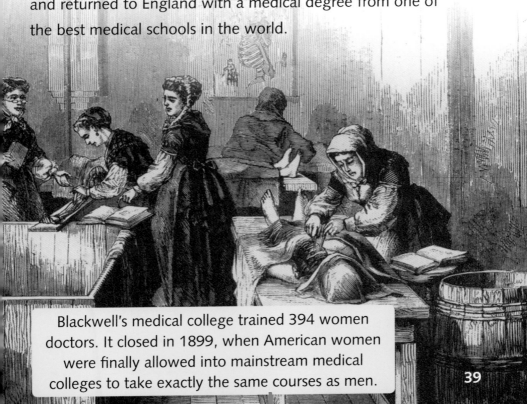

Blackwell's medical college trained 394 women doctors. It closed in 1899, when American women were finally allowed into mainstream medical colleges to take exactly the same courses as men.

# THE LONDON SCHOOL OF MEDICINE FOR WOMEN

In 1869, Elizabeth Blackwell left her sister Emily in charge of their New York hospital and medical school, and moved back to England. There, she teamed up with Elizabeth Garrett Anderson and Sophia Jex-Blake, who was the third registered female doctor in Britain, to set up a women's medical school in London.

The London School of Medicine for Women opened in 1874, with Blackwell and Garrett Anderson among the teachers. Students could get hands-on experience in Garrett Anderson's hospital, but at first they had to go to different countries to take their exams. Thanks to campaigning by Jex-Blake and others, the law changed in 1876 allowing women to take medical exams in the UK.

Sophia Jex-Blake (1840–1912) had a very different approach to fighting for women's rights, and quarrelled with Garrett Anderson, but the doctors eventually joined forces.

The London School of Medicine for Women was the first in the UK to train female doctors. Garrett Anderson eventually became the head of the school, and ran it for 20 years.

## Wider campaigning

Elizabeth Blackwell and Elizabeth Garrett Anderson were both interested in health as well as sickness. They didn't just want to treat people – they wanted to stop them from getting ill in the first place.

## Better hygiene

Blackwell and Garrett Anderson introduced things like hand washing and regular cleaning into their hospitals. Today we know these steps are important for killing germs, but in the 1800s hygiene was a new idea. Doctors often spread disease themselves, by going straight from operations or dissections to treat new patients.

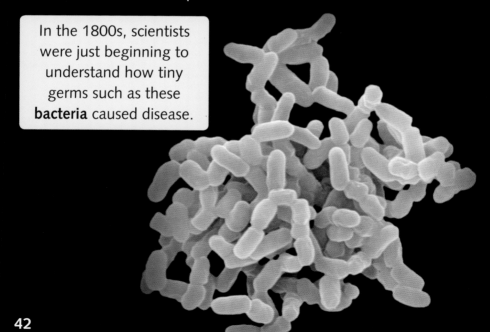

In the 1800s, scientists were just beginning to understand how tiny germs such as these **bacteria** caused disease.

## MINI-BIOGRAPHY:
# FLORENCE NIGHTINGALE
(1820–1910)

Elizabeth Blackwell was inspired by the work of her friend
Florence Nightingale. Florence Nightingale became famous for
improving conditions in army hospitals during the **Crimean War**.
After the war, Florence devoted her life to improving nursing and
hospital care. Although she was a successful woman working in
medicine, she did not like the idea of women doctors. She felt that
a focus on great nursing would improve medicine more rapidly.

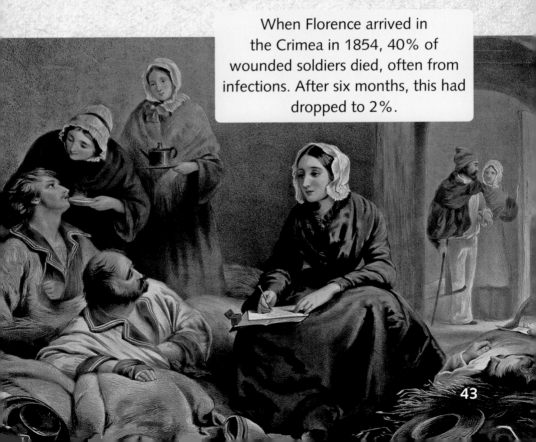

When Florence arrived in
the Crimea in 1854, 40% of
wounded soldiers died, often from
infections. After six months, this had
dropped to 2%.

## LATER LIFE

Elizabeth Blackwell and Elizabeth Garrett Anderson crushed the idea that women were too silly, too emotional or too weak to study medicine. They won the respect of doctors, patients and the public. Both women worked into their eighties, helping to make medicine – and society – a fairer place.

Blackwell helped to set up a National Health Society in England, to spread information about hygiene and healthy lifestyles. Their motto was "Prevention is better than Cure".

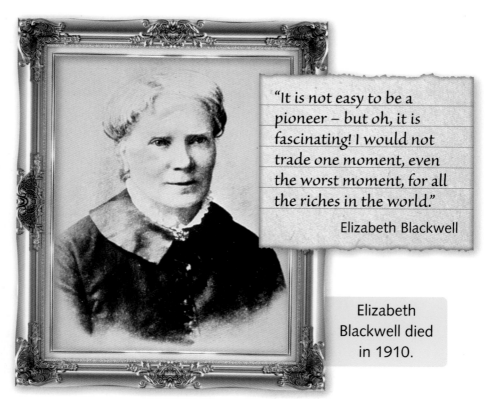

"It is not easy to be a pioneer – but oh, it is fascinating! I would not trade one moment, even the worst moment, for all the riches in the world."

Elizabeth Blackwell

Elizabeth Blackwell died in 1910.

Meanwhile, Garrett Anderson joined the struggle for women's right to vote, and became England's first female mayor, in the town where she had been born.

Elizabeth Garrett Anderson lived until she was 81 and died in 1917.

# A CHANGING WORLD

Elizabeth Blackwell and Elizabeth Garrett Anderson joined
a campaign that helped women win the right to train as doctors in
England and Wales in 1876. But female doctors still found many
obstacles in their way, and their numbers grew slowly at first.

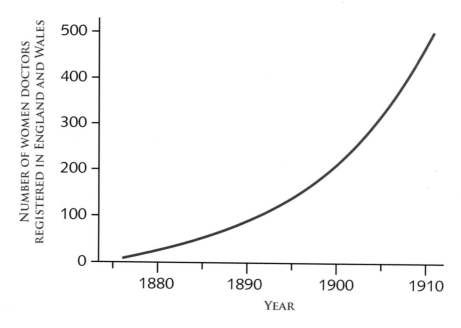

By 1900, more than 50,000 British women worked in
the medical profession, but most were nurses. There were
only 200 trained women doctors. Most medical schools did
not admit women until there was a shortage of doctors during
World War I. America's top medical schools did not admit
women until the end of World War II.

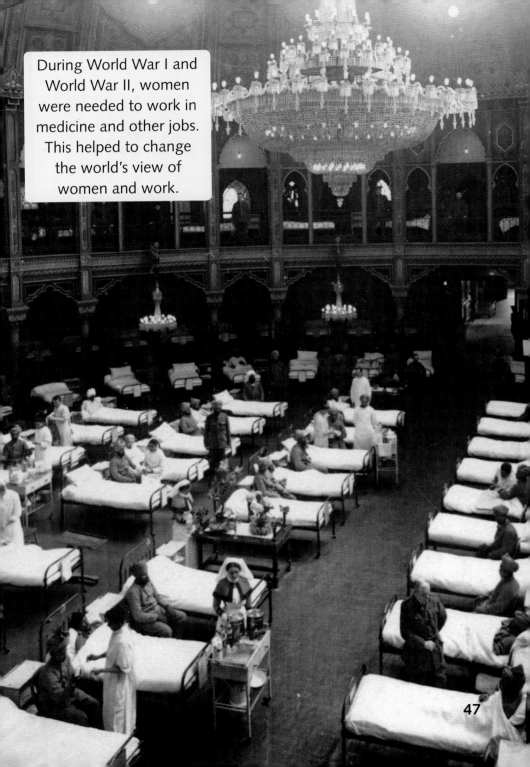

During World War I and World War II, women were needed to work in medicine and other jobs. This helped to change the world's view of women and work.

# IS THE FIGHT OVER?

The proportion of female doctors continued to rise throughout the 20th century and today, more than 60% of new medical students are women. But there are still few women in certain types of medicine, such as surgery.

Medicine was the first profession to let women in. It took longer for women to win the fight to be lawyers, architects, accountants and civil servants, and there are still fewer women working in these areas today.

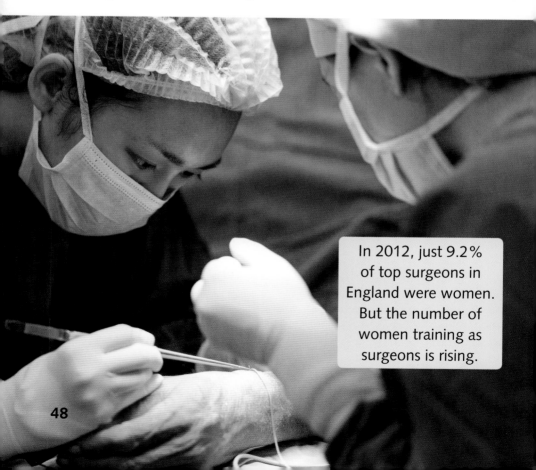

In 2012, just 9.2% of top surgeons in England were women. But the number of women training as surgeons is rising.

# Mini-biography:
# Gertrude Belle Elion

(1918–1999)

During the 20th century, women began to shape the world of medicine as scientists, too. When Gertrude Belle Elion's grandfather died of cancer, she decided to become a scientist and join the search for a cure. At first, she faced a battle – the colleges where medical researchers trained did not want to fund a woman. Gertrude worked in different jobs to pay for her own training. In the 1940s, she finally became a scientist. Her work on cancer-fighting drugs won her the Nobel Prize in Medicine in 1988.

## "THE MOST COMPLETE FREEDOM"

In 2011, one of the world's most powerful women, Michelle Obama, spoke to girls from a London school named after Elizabeth Garrett Anderson. She told them that if they worked hard, they could become anything they wanted. She also asked them "to reach back and to help others get here, too".

First Lady Michelle Obama spoke to students from the Elizabeth Garret Anderson school.

This is exactly what Elizabeth Blackwell and Elizabeth Garrett Anderson did. They thought it was wrong that medicine was a "man's job". They worked hard to kick open the hospital doors. Once inside, they improved healthcare for women. By setting up training hospitals, they helped others to follow in their footsteps.

Their achievements helped to create societies where women can follow their dreams, and choose how they spend their lives.

> "I do not wish to give [women] a first place, still less a second one – but the most complete freedom, to take their true place whatever it may be."
>
> Elizabeth Blackwell

Blackwell and Garrett Anderson are remembered by institutions named in their honour.

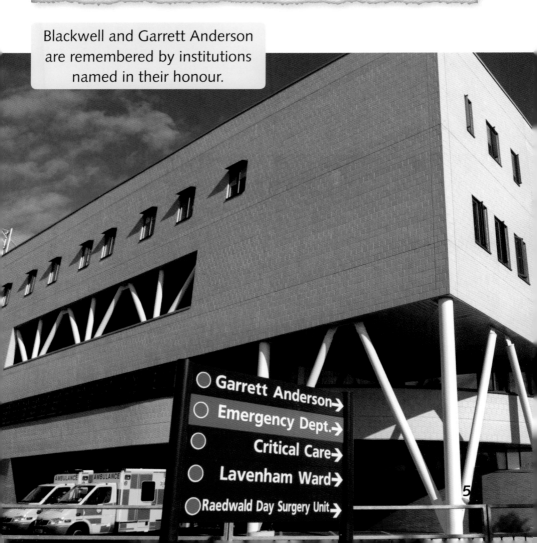

○ **Garrett Anderson→**
○ **Emergency Dept.→**
○
   **Critical Care→**
○ **Lavenham Ward→**
○Raedwald Day Surgery Unit→

5

# GLOSSARY

| | |
|---|---|
| **anatomy** | studying how the bodies of humans and other animals are made |
| **archaeologists** | people who study how humans lived in the past, by digging up buried clues |
| **bacteria** | tiny living thing, made up of just one cell; some can cause disease |
| **campaigning** | series of actions, planned and carried out to achieve a goal |
| **cholera** | a deadly disease caused by bacteria in dirty water |
| **Crimean War** | three-year war (1853–1856) between Russia and other countries including Britain and Turkey |
| **dissection** | cutting up dead bodies to learn about how they work |
| **frivolous** | silly or foolish |
| **hygiene** | methods of keeping clean to avoid spreading disease |
| **Infirmary** | another name for hospital |
| **leeches** | types of worm with suckers |
| **medical licence** | official document saying a person is allowed to work as a doctor |
| **midwifery** | the work done by people who are trained to help women give birth |
| **modesty** | not wanting to behave incorrectly |
| **perseverance** | keep doing something that is difficult or takes a long time |
| **vote** | make a choice by asking lots of people to say what their decision is, and picking the option with the highest number of yeses |

# INDEX

# THE CAREERS OF ELIZABETH BLACKWELL AND ELIZABETH GARRETT ANDERSON

**1847**
Elizabeth Blackwell enters medical school in America

**1857**
Elizabeth Blackwell, Emily Blackwell and Maria Zakrzewska open the New York Infirmary for Women and Children

**1840**

**1850**

**1849**
Elizabeth Blackwell qualifies as a doctor in America

**1853**
Elizabeth Blackwell opens her own clinic in New York

**1868**
Elizabeth Blackwell opens a medical school for women

**1874**
Elizabeth Blackwell, Elizabeth Garrett Anderson and Sophia Jex-Blake help to set up the London School of Medicine for Women

**1859**
Elizabeth Blackwell inspires Elizabeth Garrett Anderson to become a doctor

**1865**
Elizabeth Garrett Anderson is awarded a medical licence

**1876**
Law is changed to allow universities to award medical degrees to women

**1860**

**1870**

**1866**
Elizabeth Garrett Anderson opens St Mary's dispensary

# Ideas for reading

Written by Clare Dowdall, PhD
*Lecturer and Primary Literacy Consultant*

**Reading objectives:**
- make comparisons within books
- check that the book makes sense to them, discussing their understanding and exploring the meaning of words in context
- summarise the main ideas drawn from more than one paragraph, identifying key details that support the main ideas

**Spoken language objectives:**
- participate in discussions, presentations, performances, role play, improvisations and debates

**Curriculum links:** History – social history; Citizenship

**Resources:** ICT for research; Materials for designing an advert

## Build a context for reading

- Look at the front cover. Ask children what they know about doctors in history and nowadays? What different sorts of work do doctors do now?

- Read the blurb together. Establish that Queen Victoria took the throne almost 200 years ago in 1837. Discuss how women were viewed in these times and why they might have been thought of as too weak to learn about medicine.

- Note that this is a dual biography. Check that children know what a biography is and identify the doctors featured: Elizabeth Garrett Anderson and Elizabeth Blackwell.

## Understand and apply reading strategies

- Look at the contents and ask children to read the headings in pairs, discussing what each heading might mean.

- Turn to pp2–3. Ask pairs to read the content to find out and note the key information. Ask for volunteers to model how they find and extract the key information (by skimming, scanning and making inferences and deductions) using all the information provided.